Benjamin Franklin

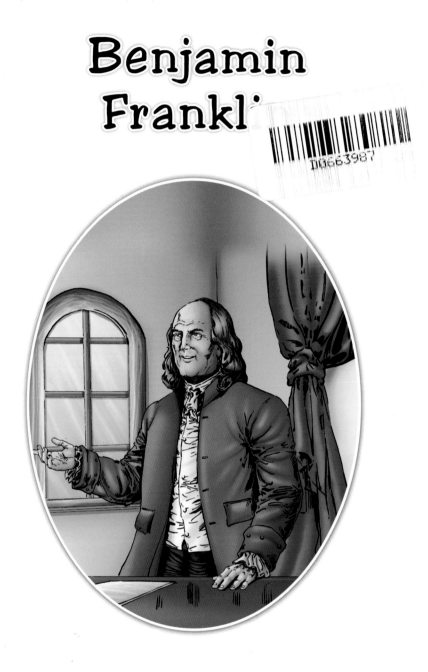

SADDLEBACK
EDUCATIONAL PUBLISHING

Saddleback's Graphic Biographies

SADDLEBACK
EDUCATIONAL PUBLISHING
www.sdlback.com

ISBN-10: 1-59905-217-2
ISBN-13: 978-1-59905-217-5
eBook: 978-1-60291-580-0

Printed in Malaysia

21 20 19 18 17   6 7 8 9 10

Benjamin Franklin was a great American. During his long and useful life he played many roles—printer, writer, inventor, scientist, good citizen, statesman, diplomat, humanitarian.

PRINTER

PUBLISHER

DIPLOMAT

POOR RICHARD'S ALMANAC

STATESMAN

WRITER

GOOD CITIZEN

INVENTOR

SCIENTIST

Benjamin Franklin was born January 17, 1706, in the city of Boston, Massachusetts.

My tenth son and fifteenth child, how wonderful!

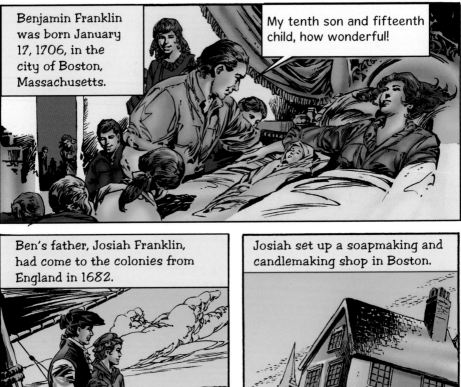

Ben's father, Josiah Franklin, had come to the colonies from England in 1682.

Josiah set up a soapmaking and candlemaking shop in Boston.

When Ben was eight, his father sent him to grammar school.

You read very well. Your writing is good. But your arithmetic is poor.

I love to read. I cannot remember when I could not read.

But his father only had enough money to let Ben go to school for two years.

I'm sorry, but money is scarce. You will have to help me now.

Ben did not like making soap or candles, so his father showed him other crafts.

I do not like this kind of work, father.

What Ben really loved was the sea and swimming.

I knew these paddles would work! I'll make some for my feet too.

Ben, you are always inventing something.

Josiah Franklin was afraid that Ben might run off to sea. So when he was twelve he apprenticed* him to his brother, James, who was 21 and had his own printing shop.

This says that I cannot drink in taverns, play unlawful games of chance, or get married while I am working for you.

The agreement also stated that James had to provide food, clothing, washing, and lodging for Ben, as well as teach him the printing trade.

Ben had to wash, sort, and set the type.

Work the press.

And deliver the newspapers each Thursday.

* to work for another to learn a skill or trade

When James Franklin started the *New England Courant,* Boston already had two newspapers. Both of them were very dull.

We need some lively articles that will make people think!

I'll sign the name Silence Dogood.

Ben knew his brother wouldn't let him write for the paper, so he wrote an article and signed it Silence Dogood. He slipped it under the door of the shop.

James liked the article and printed it.

Whoever did this is better than any of us.

Ben wrote thirteen more articles under the name of Silence Dogood. James printed them, and the readers loved them. But when Ben admitted that he was the author, James was very angry. He told Ben his job was to work the presses, not to write.

Some of James' articles criticized the government. He was jailed for one month.

This is unfair! There is no such thing as public liberty without freedom of speech.

To prevent having his paper supervised by the government, James published his paper under Ben's name.

I will look up your apprentice agreement. We can make a new secret agreement.

But James still would not let Ben write for the paper. Ben was very unhappy.

I am going to run away. I'll sell my books and buy a boat ticket to New York.

It took Ben three days to get there.

There was only one printer in New York. He had no work for a journeyman printer.*
So Ben took a boat to New Jersey.

* an experienced and reliable worker after having been an apprentice

He walked fifty miles across New Jersey in the rain. When he reached the Delaware River, Ben had only a dollar and a shilling left.

I'm glad I've read so much. Now I have something to think about.

He helped some men row a boat down the river to Philadelphia.

You don't need to give me any of your money. You helped row.

Sometimes a man is more generous when he has so little. Please keep it.

Ben bought three pennies worth of bread at the bakery and got three large, puffy rolls.

The young lady watching from the doorway was Deborah Read, Ben's future wife.

He gave away two loaves of bread to a woman and her child. It was Sunday. Ben followed a group of Quakers to their meetinghouse.

Tired from his hard traveling, he soon fell fast asleep inside.

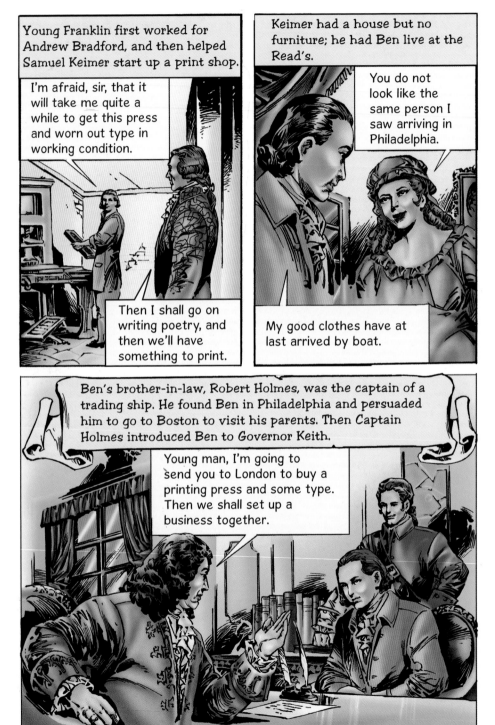

In London, Franklin learned that Governor Keith was a dreamer, who had no money or credit. So Ben worked for eighteen months as a journeyman printer. He loved London.

He was thrilled with the great variety of books.

I say that those who disagree with the church should be able to worship as they please!

He was stirred by the exciting conversations in the taverns.

He enjoyed going to the theater and to lectures.

That young colonist swims like a fish!

And he taught many admiring Englishmen how to swim.

The trip back to the colonies took fifty-one days. Ben took notes of his observations of sea life, marine vegetation, and eclipses.

Back in Philadelphia, Keimer again hired Ben, but this time at a large salary.

We have made the first type ever cast in the colonies and not imported from England.

But Ben and Keimer did not get along.

Now that I have trained the apprentices, Keimer no longer wants to pay me so much money.

My father will buy us our own print shop, and we will be partners.

Ben worked very hard. When he bought paper for the new shop, he took it through the streets in a wheelbarrow.

A penny saved is two pence clear.

He soon bought out his partner. In 1729 he published the *Pennsylvania Gazette,* which became one of the foremost American newspapers.

That Franklin is clever. See, he's illustrated this news story with a map.

In 1730 at the age of 24, Benjamin Franklin married Deborah Read. They were married for 45 years.

A man who owes money is a slave to his creditor. With your help, dear Debbie, we will add a bookstore to the print shop for added income.

We can sell many things, ointment and soap your brothers make. And coffee, tea, chocolate, cheese, codfish ...

Franklin had even more work when the Pennsylvania Assembly named him official printer.

I am going to print a better almanac* under the name of Richard Saunders.

It will be called *Poor Richard's Almanac.* I'll fill all the spaces between important dates with little bits of wisdom.

Poor Richard's Almanac was published for 26 years and was one of the most popular books in America.

Early to bed and early to rise, makes a man healthy, wealthy, and wise.

And listen to this: *God helps those who help themselves.*

* an almanac is published yearly and includes a calendar, important dates, weather information, and the rising and setting times of the sun and moon

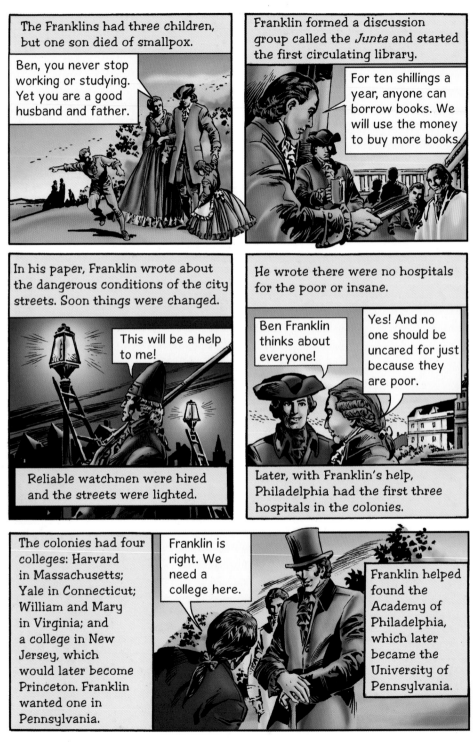

The Franklins had three children, but one son died of smallpox.

Ben, you never stop working or studying. Yet you are a good husband and father.

Franklin formed a discussion group called the *Junta* and started the first circulating library.

For ten shillings a year, anyone can borrow books. We will use the money to buy more books.

In his paper, Franklin wrote about the dangerous conditions of the city streets. Soon things were changed.

This will be a help to me!

Reliable watchmen were hired and the streets were lighted.

He wrote there were no hospitals for the poor or insane.

Ben Franklin thinks about everyone!

Yes! And no one should be uncared for just because they are poor.

Later, with Franklin's help, Philadelphia had the first three hospitals in the colonies.

The colonies had four colleges: Harvard in Massachusetts; Yale in Connecticut; William and Mary in Virginia; and a college in New Jersey, which would later become Princeton. Franklin wanted one in Pennsylvania.

Franklin is right. We need a college here.

Franklin helped found the Academy of Philadelphia, which later became the University of Pennsylvania.

Fire losses in Philadelphia were alarmingly high.

Heaven help us if I drop any sparks and don't see them.

Franklin published an article pointing out that there was no order in fighting fires.

An ounce of prevention is worth a pound of cure. Planning not to have fires is easier than fighting them.

In 1736 Benjamin Franklin organized the Union Fire Company. Every member was required to have a leather bucket for water and a basket to remove goods from a fire.

We will have a meeting once each month to talk about fires. If you do not attend you will be fined, and we will use the money for new equipment.

The chief directs the opening of the roofs by axmen and the pulling down of timbers by hook men. He appoints guards to watch goods moved out of burning buildings.

For six years France and Spain were at war with England. The struggle spread to the colonies.

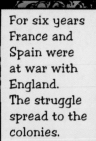

In 1747 Franklin wrote a pamphlet called *Plain Truth*. In it he described what might happen to the city if it was attacked.

The pamphlet made the people think seriously about the war.

Franklin called a mass meeting and organized a voluntary association for the defense of the city.

I hear that Franklin borrowed eighteen cannons from New York Governor Clinton.

In 1737 Franklin was named postmaster of Philadelphia. In 1753 he became deputy postmaster general for all the colonies. He introduced many reforms.

We need a city delivery system and a dead letter office.

We need better routes and more men to ride both night and day.

We're the fastest ship available, sir. We'll deliver your mail to Europe.

In 1763 Franklin helped Canada open post offices in Québec, Montreal, and Trois Rivières.

In 1748 at the age of forty-two, Benjamin Franklin retired as a publisher. He wanted to read, study, and make experiments.

He invented many, many items, but never took out a patent or used them to make a profit. He believed that ideas should be shared.

The Franklin stove made a room twice as warm with one-fourth the amount of fuel.

By using bifocals, a person could look from near objects to distant ones without changing glasses.

A metal rod with its lower end in the ground directed a lightning flash harmlessly into the earth.

He made many discoveries and shared his findings with other scientists.

He favored daylight savings.

He was the first scientist to study the movement of the Gulf Stream.

It is foolish that people live much by candlelight and sleep by sunshine.

He showed America how to improve acidic soil by adding lime.

We need to study the speed, temperature, and depth.

In 1752 Franklin flew a kite into a thunderstorm and proved that lightning and the feeble electric sparks scientist produced was the same thing.

This is a dangerous experiment if not done properly.

Franklin's descriptions of plus and minus charges, and his other writing on electricity, were translated into French, German, and Italian.

But no practical use had been found for electricity. It was often used on the stage to amuse people.

You are seeing pure magic.

Benjamin Franklin was one of the best educated men of his times, even though he went to school for only two years. He studied mathematics and all the known natural and physical sciences.

This makes me very happy.

He received honorary degrees from Harvard, Yale, William and Mary, St. Andrews, and Oxford. He had the rare honor of being elected a member of the Royal Society of London and the French Academy of Sciences. He was president of the American Philosophical Society, which he helped found, until his death.

In the spring of 1754 war broke out between the British and French in America. The Indians fought alongside the French.

Franklin felt the colonies had to unite for self-defense.

JOIN, or DIE

In his paper, Franklin published the first political cartoons.

Representatives of the northern colonies met in Albany, New York. Franklin was a delegate from Pennsylvania.

We must work together or we shall be overcome!

He wrote the royalist governor of Massachusetts that the colonists would not obey tax laws made in England. He also wrote that the English trade laws were unfair to the colonists.

This man talks of revolution.

These ideas became the battle cries of the Revolution.

Benjamin Franklin also suggested that new colonies be formed west of the Appalachian Mountains for the growing number of Americans.

America's future will depend on the West.

The first territory was named Franklin in his honor, but the name was later changed to Tennessee.

In November 1754 the Shawnee attacked a Pennsylvania village, 75 miles from Philadelphia.

Governor Morris sent Franklin to arrange defenses on the frontier.

We are prepared. The women help defend us by throwing stones.

Franklin was not a military man, but with the help of a book of instructions and a group of axmen, he directed the building of three forts.

Back in Philadelphia, Franklin was appointed colonel and put in charge of the city's militia, supported by British regulars.

Please hold your fire. All right men! Ready, aim, fire!

The British sent over General Braddock with two regiments.

General Braddock, I can get you the horses and wagons you need. The people know me and trust me.

But Braddock did not know how to fight against Native Americans. Sixty-three of his 86 officers were killed, and 714 out of 1,100 men.

How can you shoot back when you can't see them?

The remaining troops refused to stay and guard the frontier and retreated to Philadelphia.

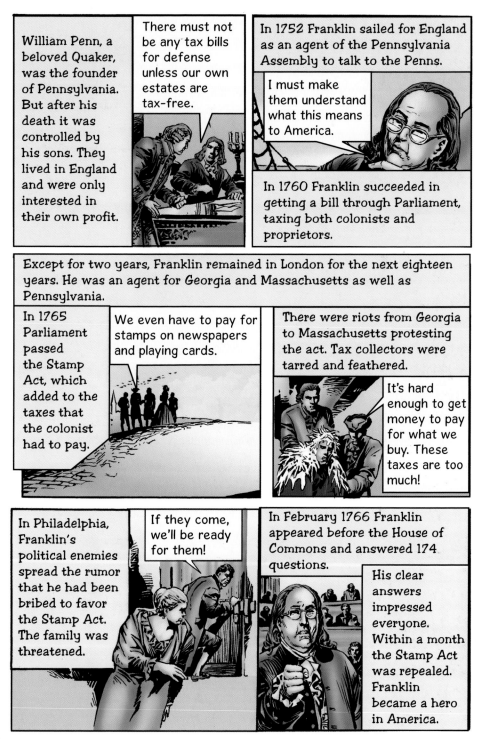

William Penn, a beloved Quaker, was the founder of Pennsylvania. But after his death it was controlled by his sons. They lived in England and were only interested in their own profit.

There must not be any tax bills for defense unless our own estates are tax-free.

In 1752 Franklin sailed for England as an agent of the Pennsylvania Assembly to talk to the Penns.

I must make them understand what this means to America.

In 1760 Franklin succeeded in getting a bill through Parliament, taxing both colonists and proprietors.

Except for two years, Franklin remained in London for the next eighteen years. He was an agent for Georgia and Massachusetts as well as Pennsylvania.

In 1765 Parliament passed the Stamp Act, which added to the taxes that the colonist had to pay.

We even have to pay for stamps on newspapers and playing cards.

There were riots from Georgia to Massachusetts protesting the act. Tax collectors were tarred and feathered.

It's hard enough to get money to pay for what we buy. These taxes are too much!

In Philadelphia, Franklin's political enemies spread the rumor that he had been bribed to favor the Stamp Act. The family was threatened.

If they come, we'll be ready for them!

In February 1766 Franklin appeared before the House of Commons and answered 174 questions.

His clear answers impressed everyone. Within a month the Stamp Act was repealed. Franklin became a hero in America.

British trade acts required that the colonists sell raw goods to England at low cost and buy back manufactured goods at high prices.

One dark night in Boston Harbor, some men dressed as Native Americans, boarded three ships and threw $50,000 worth of tea into the water.

Franklin offered to pay for the tea destroyed at the Boston Tea Party with his own money. But he said the British must stop the tax on tea. They paid no attention to his offer.

I agree that some of these taxes are not right.

Governor Hutchinson of Massachusetts wrote letters to England suggesting that force be used to put down the colonists.

Those rascals need to be taught a good lesson!

By mistake, Benjamin Franklin was given the letters.

Franklin sent the letters to Sam Adams in Massachusetts, who read them in a secret meeting.

And Hutchinson himself would like to see us brought to our knees.

King George III and his ministers repealed some bad taxes but refused to repeal the tax on tea.

The British were angry when the letters became public. Franklin was called before the King's Privy Council. He was accused of being the chief troublemaker between England and the American colonies.

But sirs, we only ask to have a say in the way we are taxed.

Franklin sailed for home in March 1775. His wife died while he was still in England. And feelings between England and America were even worse than before.

In Lexington and Concord, on April 19, 1775, fighting broke out between British Redcoats and American Patriots. Franklin was only midway across the Atlantic.

Yet Franklin continued to be interested in everything around him. While sailing home, he made a chart of the Gulf Stream.

Franklin arrived home on May 5 and the next day was made a delegate to the Second Continental Congress.

Franklin may be the oldest delegate, but he is certainly one of the busiest.

He was on the committee to help draft the Declaration of Independence. He was one of the signers of that famous document.

I think Jefferson was chosen to do the writing for fear I would add a joke or proverb.

The war was going badly for the Americans in 1776. Franklin was sent to France to try to get their help.

He acts as though he doesn't know the danger we are in from British patrols.

In France, Franklin received a wonderful welcome. Noblemen and common people alike loved him.

He seems interested only in the sea life and the Gulf Stream.

He is a simple man, but a great man!

He is becoming so popular that soon his picture will hang in most French homes.

Franklin talked to everyone about America's need for French help and friendship.

If America wins this war, think of all the trade that France would have with us.

Sir, you talk like one of us.

He pointed out to government officials how powerful the rival British would be if they won the war.

Sire, if the colonies are defeated, England will become too powerful.

In 1778 an alliance with France was signed. Franklin was one of the signers.

During the war, it was Benjamin Franklin's main task to get loans and gifts of money for the Americans.

He also had to select foreign officers who wanted to serve in the Continental Army.

Baron Von Steuben soon turned Washington's Valley Forge troops into a well drilled army.

The Marquis de Lafayette became one of General Washington's closest friends.

He helped John Paul Jones obtain a ship to fight the British.

We have named her *Bonhomme Richard* after *Poor Richard's Almanac.*

Fight well. But tell your commanders not to harm the English Captain Cook. He is doing scientific research.

On October 19, 1781, the British surrendered. On September 3, 1783, the Treaties of Paris, the formal peace treaties with England, France, and America, were signed. Franklin was one of the signers.

May we never see another war. There was never a good war or a bad peace.

Before leaving France, Franklin published a pamphlet for people who wanted to go to America.

America is the land of great opportunity only if you are willing to work hard.

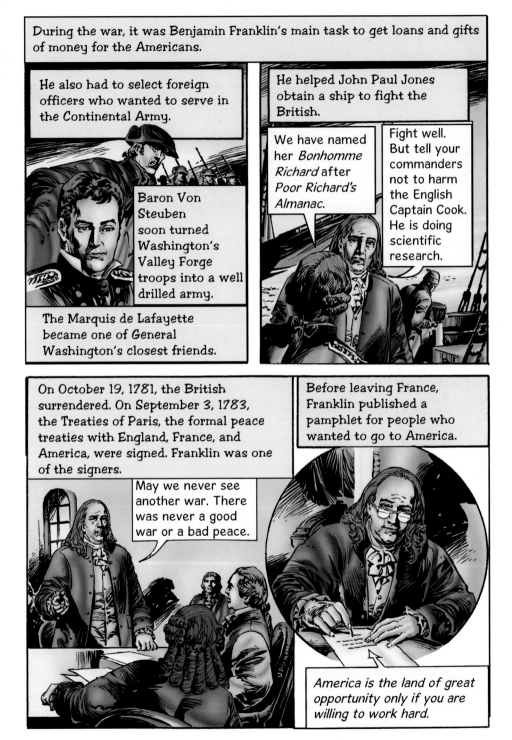

Franklin returned to Philadelphia in 1785. Cannons boomed, church bells pealed, and there were parades for a whole week.

I have been away so long I thought I had been forgotten.

But his work was not over.

He became president of the first anti-slavery society in America. In 1787 he was a delegate to the Constitutional Convention.

He helped work out a plan for the House of Representatives. Its size would depend on the number of people in each state. But the Senate would have the same number from each state.

It was Franklin's closing speech that helped make the adoption of the Constitution unanimous.

In his final years, Franklin continued work on his autobiography and kept on inventing many useful things.

See how I can take down books from the high shelves ...

His son William had remained loyal to the British and lived in England. Franklin lived with his loving daughter, Sally, and her children.

Eight grandchildren, I am indeed blessed.

He died on April 17, 1790, at the age of 84.

Benjamin Franklin's face is on postage stamps and money. He also designed the Fugio copper cent. The first coin made by the United States.

Two presidents were named after him: Franklin Pierce and Franklin Delano Roosevelt.

Franklin Institute in Philadelphia is dedicated to aiding science.

It contains a reconstruction of his printing shop with his own printing press.

He was the only one of the founding fathers who signed all four documents leading to the birth of an independent United States.

DECLARATION OF INDEPENDENCE

PEACE TREATY WITH ENGLAND

ALLIANCE WITH FRANCE

THE CONSTITUTION

Benjamin Franklin always worked hard. He never lost his sense of curiosity about any subject. No matter what role his country asked him to play, he never complained, but always did his best. He was a great patriot and a great man.

the END